THE GREAT BIG JOKE BOOK

© Ward Lock Limited 1987

First published in Great Britain in 1987
by Ward Lock Limited, 8 Clifford Street
London W1X 1RB, an Egmont Company

Printed and bound in Finland

Cover by Jan Sitek

British Library Cataloguing in Publication Data
Clarke, Heather
   The great big joke book for kids.
   1. Wit and humor, Juvenile   2. English wit
   and humor
   I. Title   II. Mitchell, Roy   III. Sitek, Jan
   828'.91402'0809282   PZ8.7

ISBN 0-7063-6578-X

THE GREAT BIG JOKE BOOK

WARD LOCK LIMITED · LONDON

Stupid Sid's Puzzle Page

WHICH SHAPE MATCHES THE FISH?

ANSWER: NO. ④, IF YOU CUT A FEW BITS OFF THE EDGES

SPOT THE DIFFERENCES...

CAN YOU SPOT TEN DIFFERENCES BETWEEN THE TWO DRAWINGS?

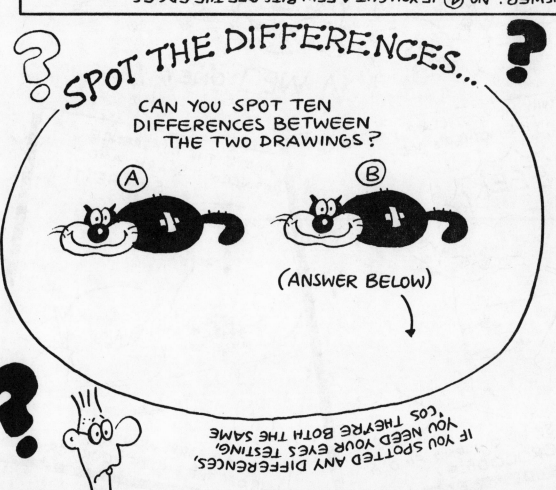

(ANSWER BELOW)

IF YOU SPOTTED ANY DIFFERENCES, YOU NEED YOUR EYES TESTING, 'COS THEY'RE BOTH THE SAME

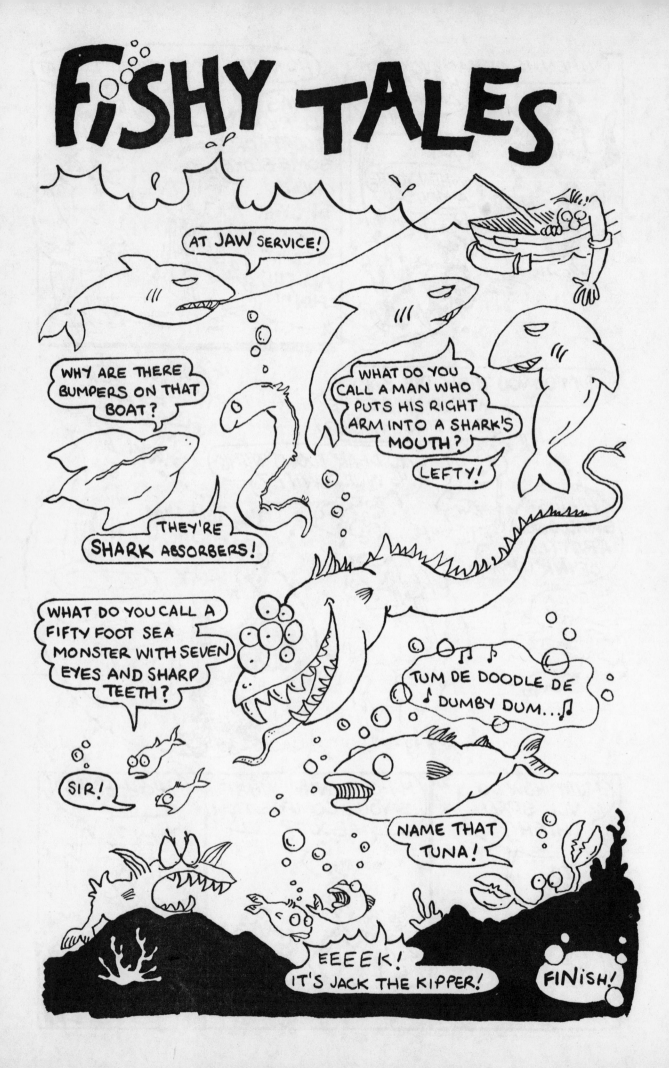

CRAZY Rhyme Time

THERE WAS A YOUNG MAN FROM LEEDS,
WHO SWALLOWED A PACKET OF SEEDS;
WITHIN JUST ONE HOUR
HIS NOSE WAS A FLOWER
AND HIS HEAD WAS A RIOT OF WEEDS!

THERE WAS A YOUNG LADY FROM RIGA,
WHO RODE WITH A SMILE ON A TIGER.
THEY RETURNED FROM THE RIDE
WITH THE LADY INSIDE,
AND THE SMILE ON THE FACE OF THE TIGER.

SILLY STRIPS

BOY MEETS GHOUL

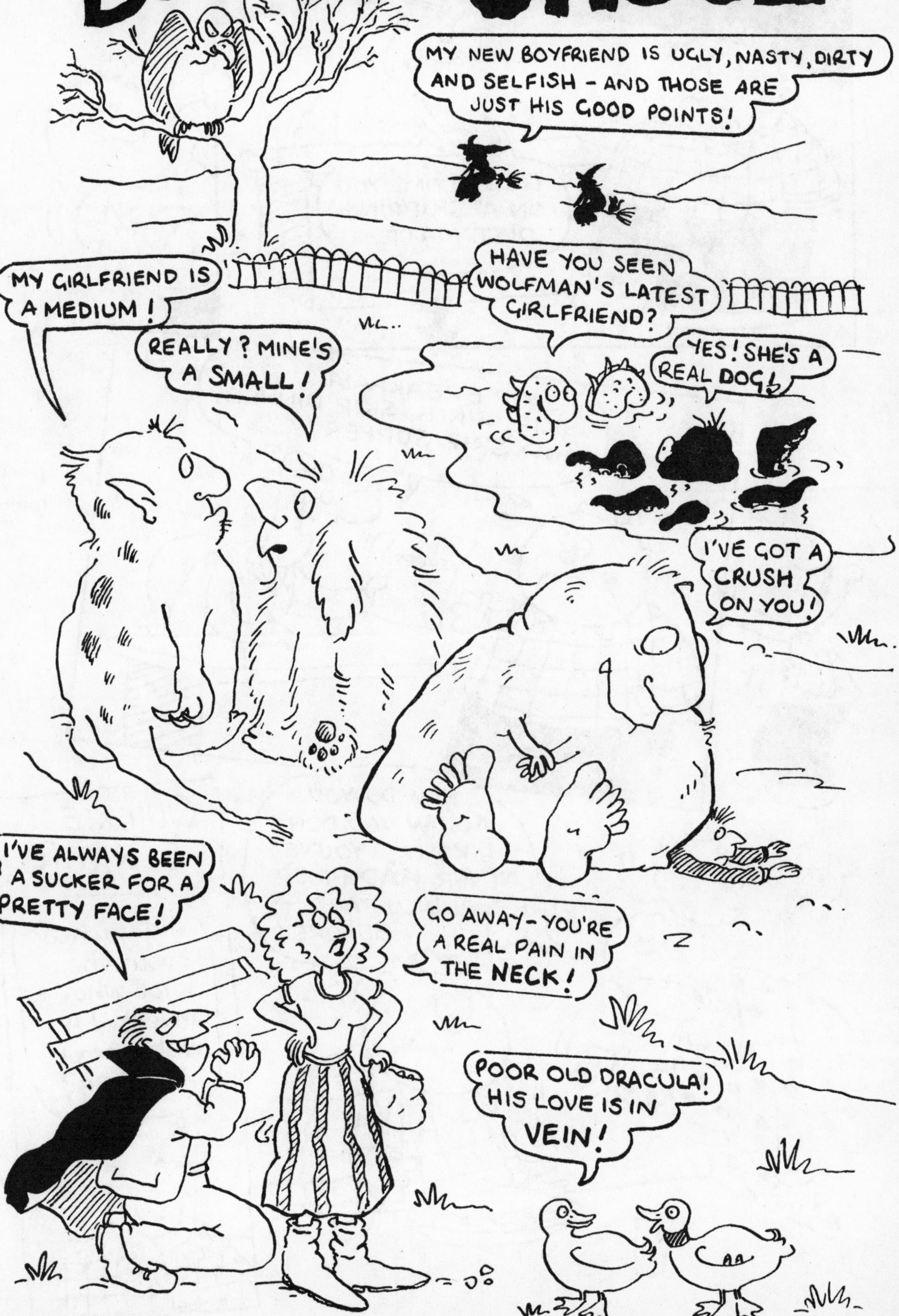

HUMPTY DUMPTY SAT ON A WALL

HUMPTY DUMPTY HAD A GREAT FALL...

...ANYONE FOR POACHED EGG?

JUST WHAT THE DOCTOR ORDERED!

SILLY STRIPS

Why did the chicken cross the road?

— FOR FOWL PURPOSES... HEH! HEH!

What did the toothpaste say to the brush?

GIVE ME A SQUEEZE AND I'LL MEET YOU OUTSIDE THE TUBE.

When would you be glad to be down and out?

AFTER A BUMPY PLANE TRIP...

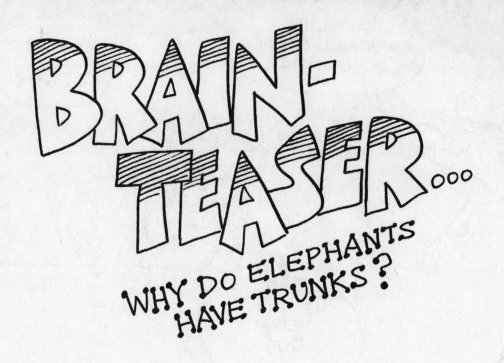

BRAIN-TEASER...

WHY DO ELEPHANTS HAVE TRUNKS?

BECAUSE THEY'D LOOK PRETTY STUPID WITH SUITCASES!

FAVOURITE NURSERY RHYMES

GEORGIE PORGIE, PUDDING AND PIE,
KISSED THE GIRLS AND MADE THEM CRY...

...NOT SURPRISING, IS IT?

DOCTOR! DOCTOR!

BOOO!GIE ON DOWN!

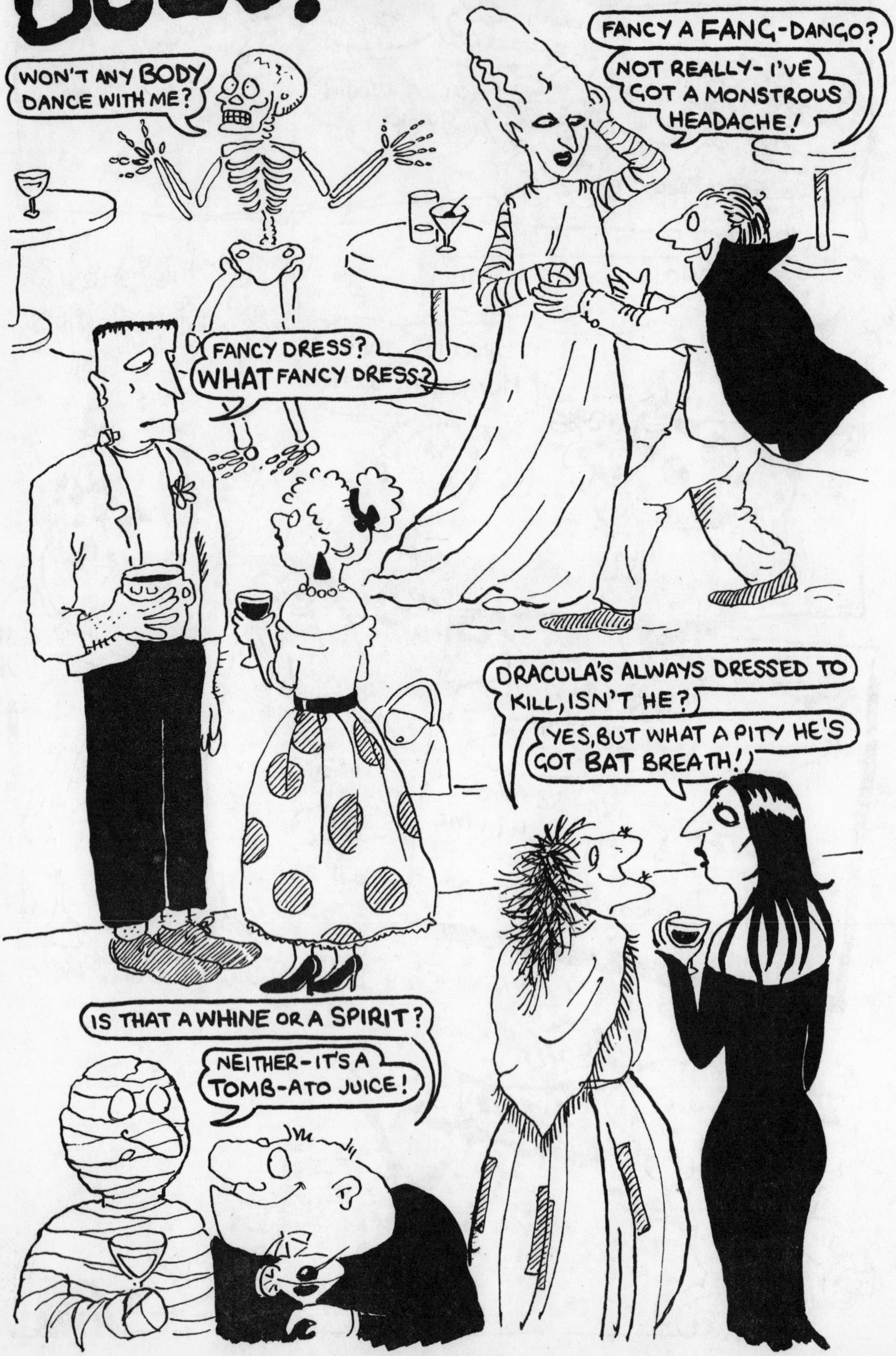

DID YOU HEAR ABOUT...

RHYME TIME

There was a young man from Quebec
Who wrapped both his legs round his neck!
But then he forgot
How to undo the knot,
And now he's an absolute wreck!

BOING!   BOING!

I eat peas with honey,
I've done it all my life.
They do taste kind of funny-
But it keeps them on the knife!

There was an old man from Whitehaven,
Whose whiskers had never been shaven;
He said, 'It is best,
For they make a nice nest,
In which I can keep my
pet raven!'

There was an old man from Penzance,
Who always wore sheet-iron pants;
He said, 'Some years back,
I sat on a tack,
And I'll never again take a chance!'

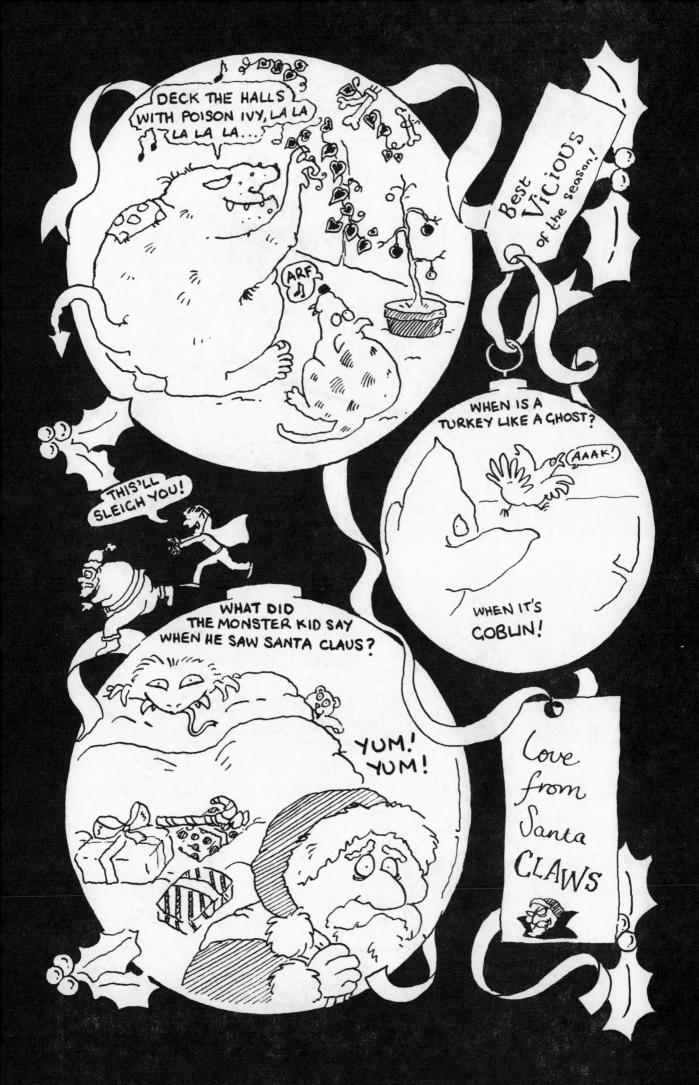

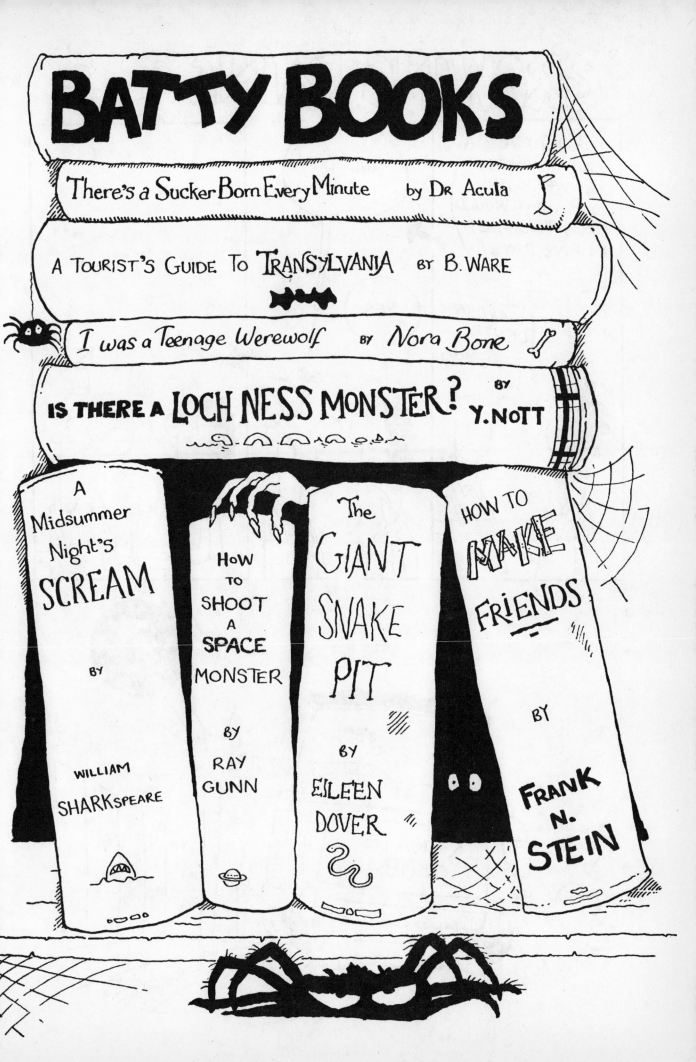

GROWING PAINS

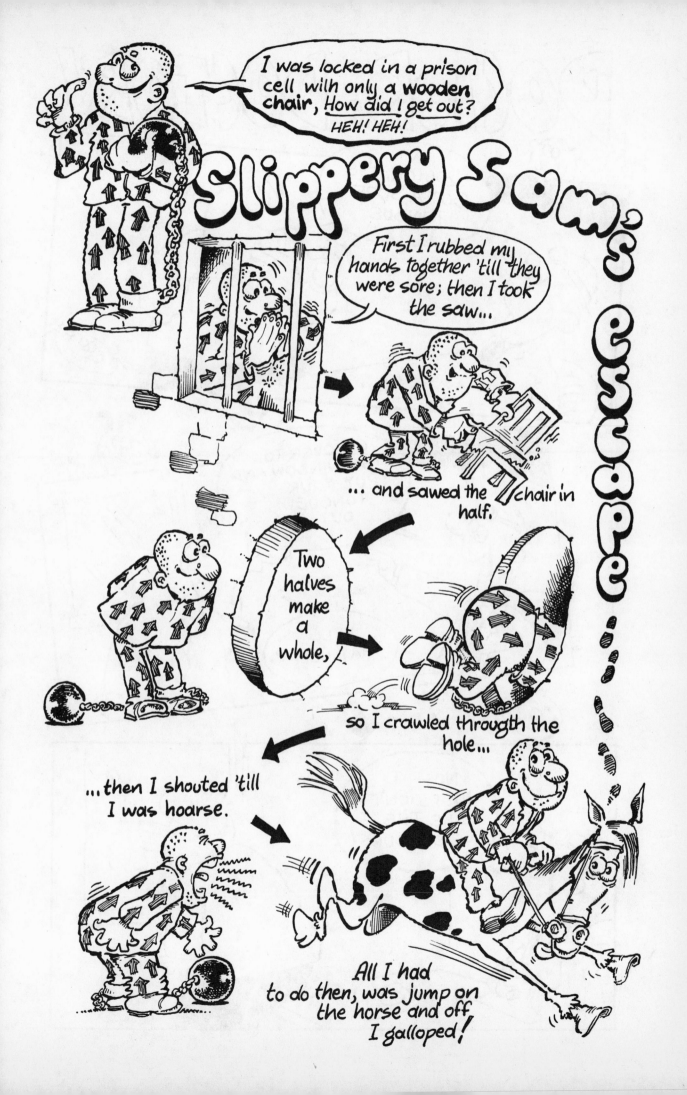

LOONY Lesson!

CRUMMY MUMMIES

QUICK PICS.

FAVOURITE NURSERY RHYMES

Old Mother Hubbard
Went to the cupboard
To fetch her poor dog a bone;
But when she got there
The cupboard was bare...

...so the dog ate Mother
Hubbard instead.

LOONY LIMERICK

A FELLOW CALLED FRED DIDN'T CARE
WHAT KIND OF CLOTHES HE'D WEAR;
HIS JACKET WAS RAGGY,
HIS TROUSERS WERE BAGGY,
AND THAT'S WHY FOLKS CALLED HIM FRED BARE!

HAPPY FAMILIES

WHAT DO YOU CALL A ONE-EYED MONSTER ON A BIKE?

CYCLE-OPS!

SHORT STORIES

What do you call a Polar bear in the desert?

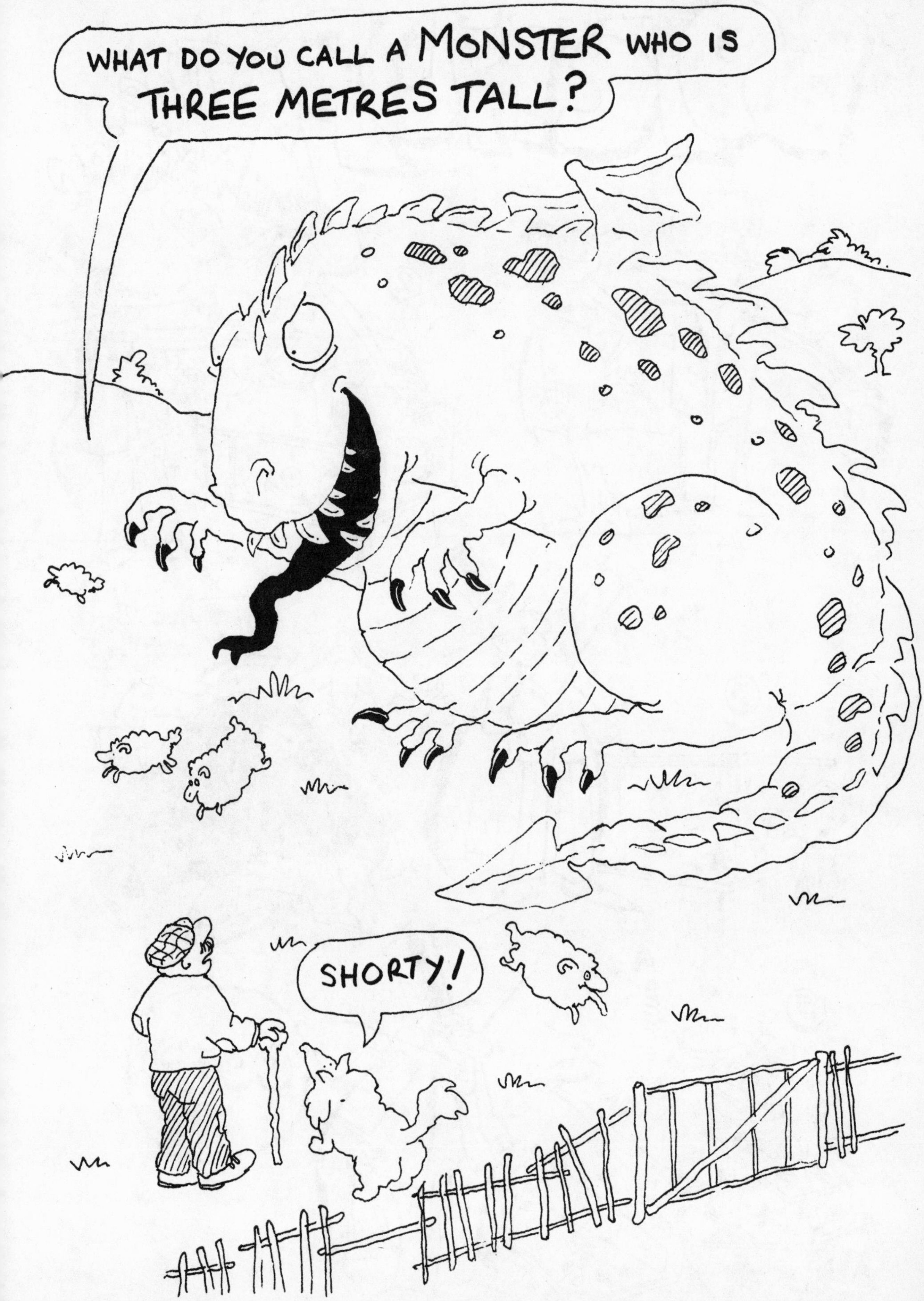
WHAT DO YOU CALL A MONSTER WHO IS THREE METRES TALL?
SHORTY!

FAVOURITE NURSERY RHYMES

Three blind mice, three blind mice.
See how they run! See how they run!
They all ran after the farmer's wife,
Who cut off their tails with a carving knife...

Next time she'll stick to roast chicken!

... language do they speak in Cuba?

← Cuban heels →

Cubic of course!!

Mommy!

WHAT CAN YOU TOUCH, SEE AND MAKE BUT CAN'T HOLD?

—YOUR SHADOW!

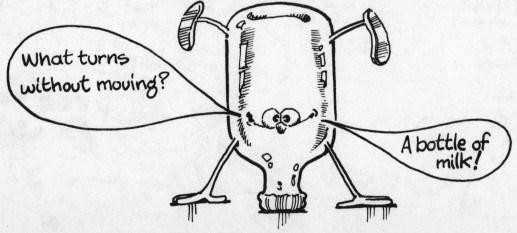

What turns without moving?

A bottle of milk!

What's Up Doc?

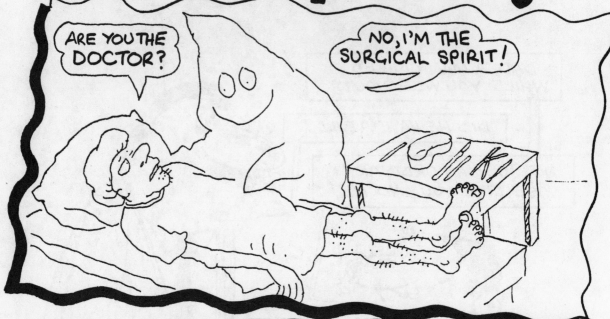

How many LEGS does a horse have?

SIX: <u>fore-legs</u> in front and two behind!

What do you get...

Stupid Sid's

~~Board~~ Game
Bored

The rules are quite simple (what else?) — all
you need are two dice, and the intelligence
of a flea. Throw a double eight to start.
First one to finish is either a genius, or as stupid
as Sid.

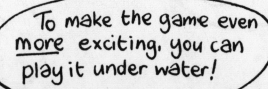

To make the game even
<u>more</u> exciting, you can
play it under water!

GHOULISH GIGGLES

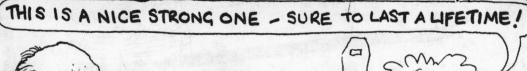

Did you hear about...

...the stupid hitch-hiker who set out early to miss the traffic?

Then there was the farmer who rolled his field because he wanted to grow mashed potatoes...

Sid's Limerick

I know a lad called Sid,
A totally stupid kid;
He gave his best hat
To a greedy cat,
Now Sid wears a dustbin lid!

Sid drops a line...

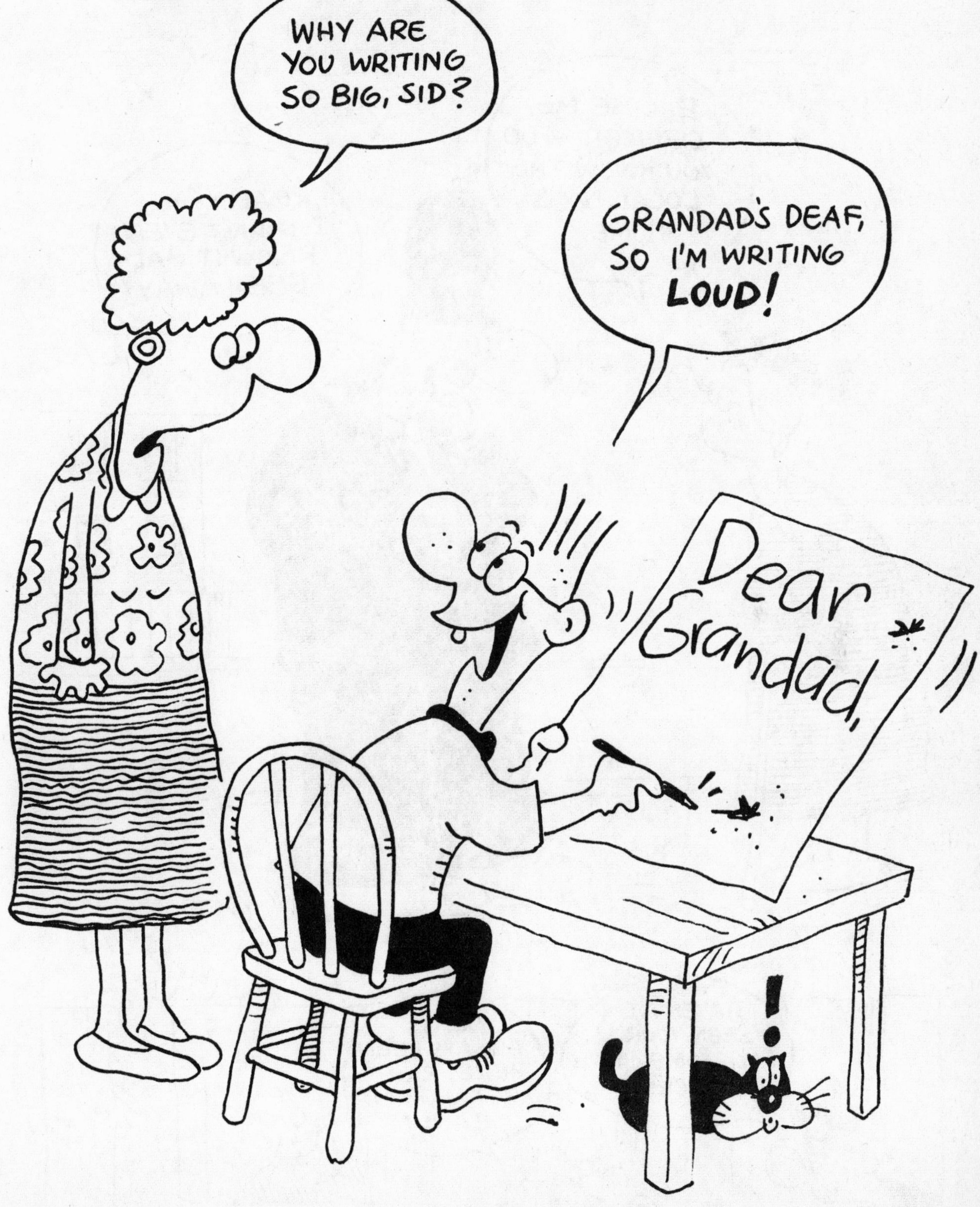

P.C. PLOP... the CRAZY COP

Have you heard the story about...

... the slippery eel? —
You wouldn't grasp it.

...the skyscraper? —
It's a tall story.

Sorry sir, the lifts out of order!

...the peacock? —
It's a beautiful tale.

Stupid Sid's
WORD SEARCH

READING UP, DOWN, ACROSS, BACK AND DIAGONALLY, CAN YOU FIND THE FOLLOWING WORDS:

SID SID SID SID SID SID
SID SID SID SID SID SID

```
S  I  D  S  I  D  S
I  D  I  S  D  I  S
D  I  S  I  I  S  I
I  D  I  D  S  D  D
S  I  D  S  I  I  S
I  S  I  D  I  S  I
D  I  S  D  S  I  D
```

(ALLOW YOURSELF 3 HOURS TO DO THIS, AS IT'S QUITE TRICKY)

WHEN THE LIGHTS
WENT OUT,
WHERE WAS
DRACULA?

IN THE DARK!

GRANDAD GETS THE MESSAGE

SCARY STORIES

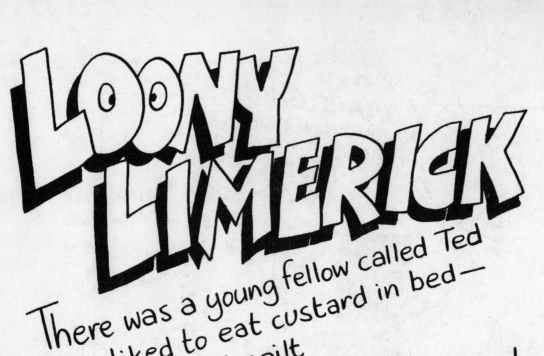

LOONY LIMERICK

There was a young fellow called Ted
Who liked to eat custard in bed—
But one day it spilt
All over his quilt,
So he ate all his bedclothes instead!

WHAT DO YOU CALL A FRIENDLY, POLITE, CLEAN, HARD-WORKING MONSTER?

A TOTAL FAILURE!

I Say, Waiter

FAVOURITE NURSERY RHYMES

HEY DIDDLE, DIDDLE,
THE CAT AND THE FIDDLE,
THE COW JUMPED OVER THE MOON;
THE LITTLE DOG LAUGHED
TO SEE SUCH FUN...

LOONY Limerick!

There was an old man called Morris
Who had a wife called Doris;
Just as he feared
She grew a beard,
So now he calls her Horace!

CREEPY

FAVOURITE NURSERY RHYMES

LITTLE MISS MUFFET
SAT ON A TUFFET
EATING HER CURDS AND WHEY;
ALONG CAME A SPIDER
WHO SAT DOWN BESIDE HER...

...SO SHE CLOBBERED IT WITH HER SPOON!

on the move

CREATURES

FAVOURITE NURSERY RHYMES

JACK AND JILL WENT UP THE HILL
TO FETCH A PAIL OF WATER;
JACK FELL DOWN
AND BROKE HIS CROWN...

...AND JILL SAID, 'YOU TWIT! NOW I'LL
HAVE TO CARRY **BOTH** BUCKETS!'